Puzzle Favorites

FIND THE 16 DIFFERENCES

Keep Score
ooooooooooooooo

FIND THE 16 DIFFERENCES

Keep Score

○○○○○○○○○○○○○○○○

FIND THE 16 DIFFERENCES

Keep Score
◦◦◦◦◦◦◦◦◦◦◦◦◦◦

FIND THE 16 DIFFERENCES

KEEP SCORE
○○○○○○○○○○○○○○○

FIND THE 16 DIFFERENCES

Keep Score
○○○○○○○○○○○○○○○

FIND THE 16 DIFFERENCES

Keep Score
○○○○○○○○○○○○○○

FIND THE 16 DIFFERENCES

Keep Score
○○○○○○○○○○○○○○○

FIND THE 16 DIFFERENCES

Keep Score
○○○○○○○○○○○○○○○○

FIND THE 16 DIFFERENCES

Keep Score
○○○○○○○○○○○○○○

Find the 16 Differences

Keep Score
ooooooooooooooo

FIND THE 16 DIFFERENCES

KEEP SCORE

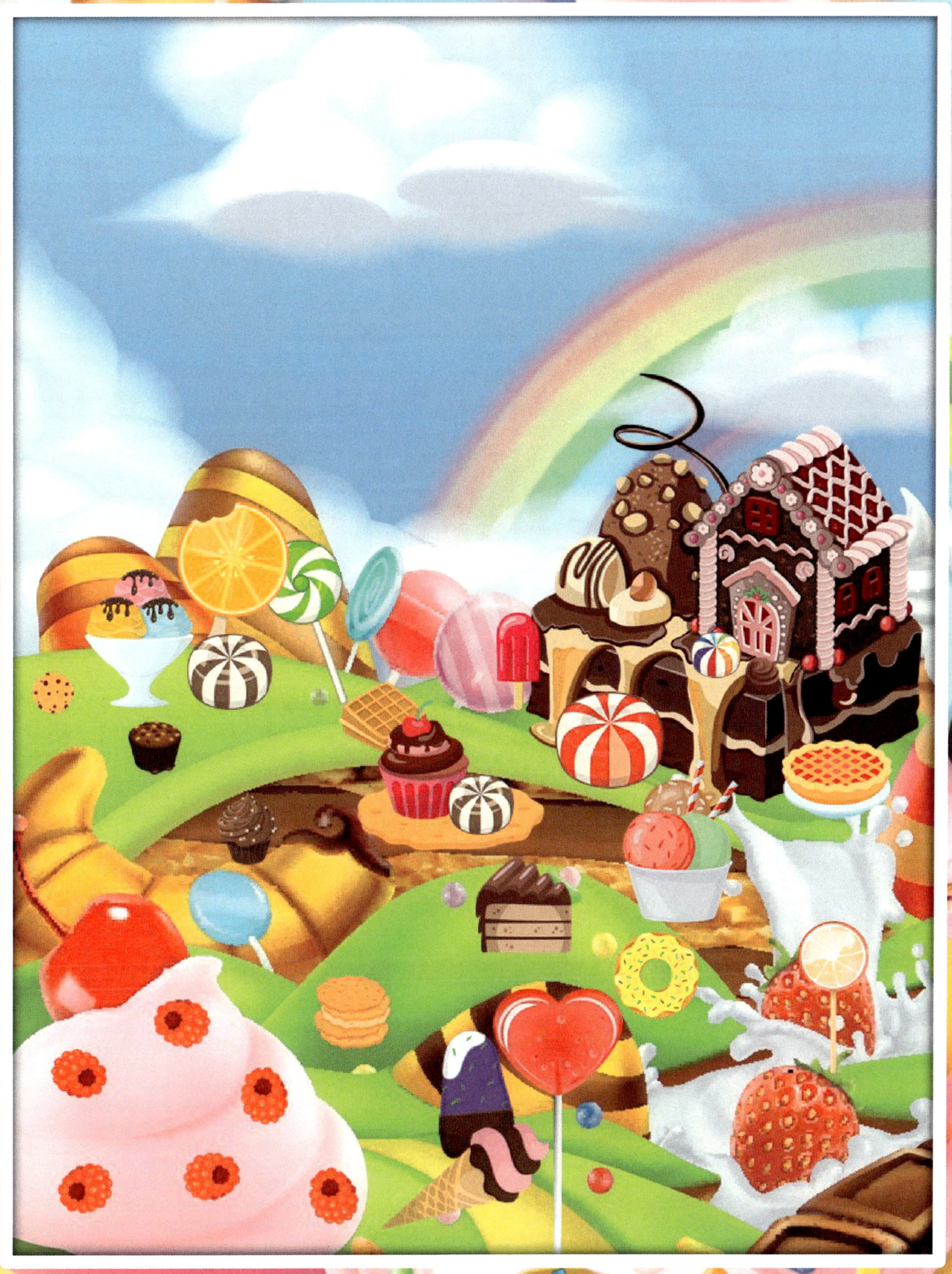

FIND THE 16 DIFFERENCES

Keep Score

ooooooooooooooooo

FIND THE 16 DIFFERENCES

Keep Score
ooooooooooooooooo

FIND THE 16 DIFFERENCES

Keep Score

○○○○○○○○○○○○○○

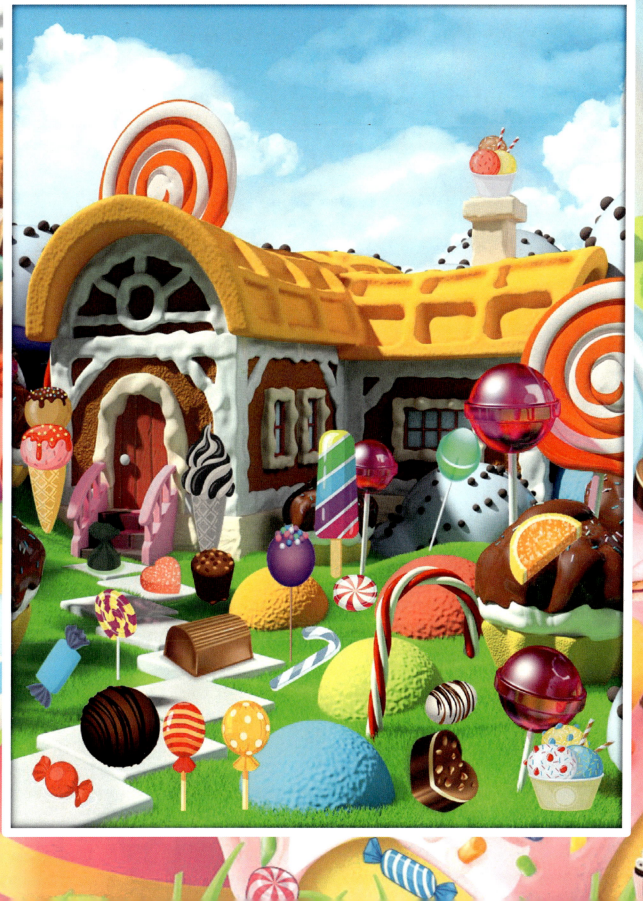

FIND THE 16 DIFFERENCES

Keep Score
○○○○○○○○○○○○○○

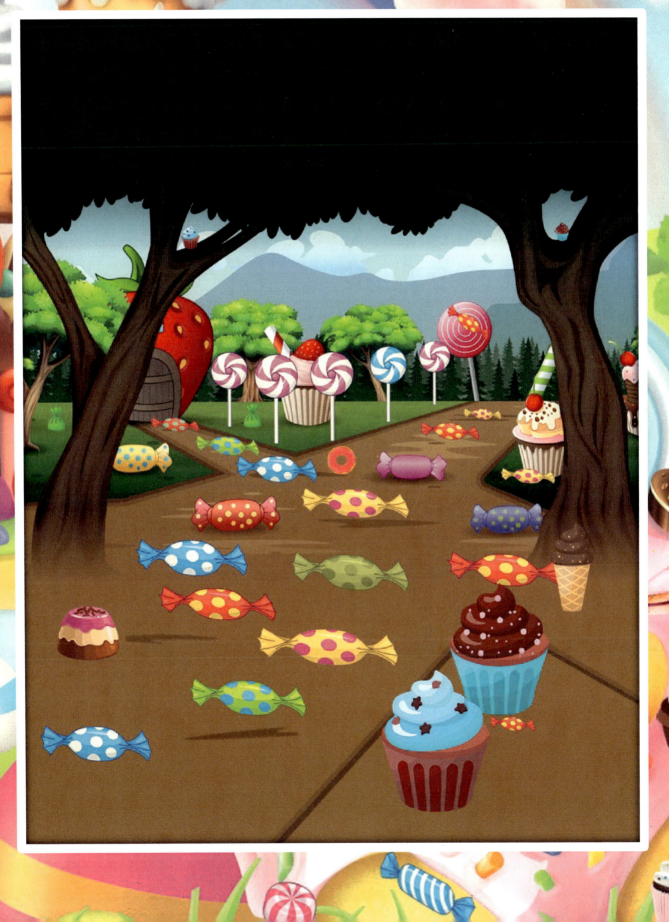

FIND THE 16 DIFFERENCES

Keep Score
ooooooooooooo

FIND THE 16 DIFFERENCES

Keep Score

○○○○○○○○○○○○○○○

FIND THE 16 DIFFERENCES

Keep Score
ooooooooooooooooo

FIND THE 16 DIFFERENCES

Keep Score
○○○○○○○○○○○○○○○

FIND THE 16 DIFFERENCES

Keep Score

FIND THE 16 DIFFERENCES

Keep Score
○○○○○○○○○○○○○○○○○○○

FIND THE 16 DIFFERENCES

Keep Score
○○○○○○○○○○○○○○○

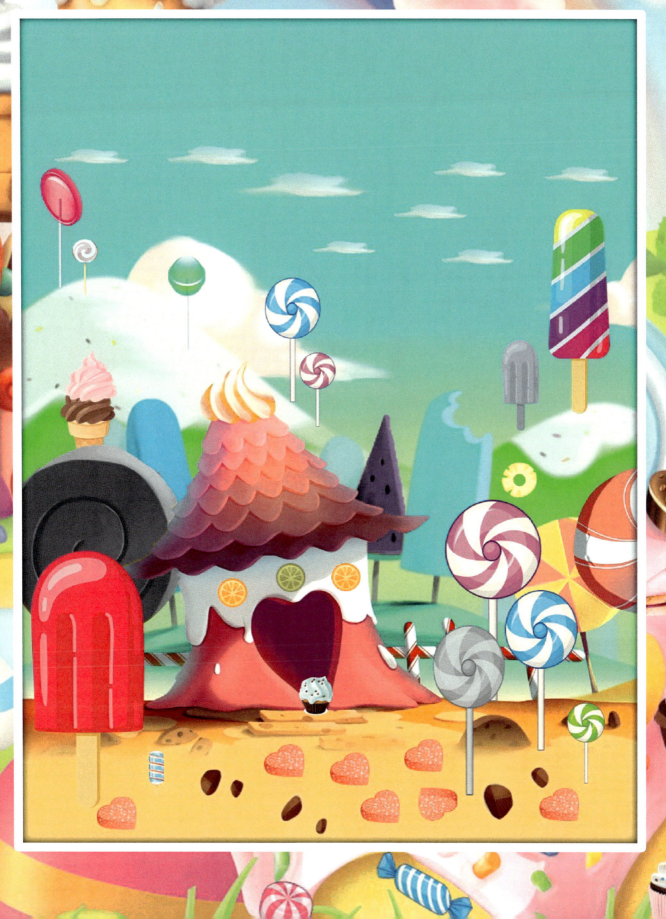

FIND THE 16 DIFFERENCES

Keep Score
○○○○○○○○○○○○○○

FIND THE 16 DIFFERENCES

Keep Score
○○○○○○○○○○○○○○○

FIND THE 16 DIFFERENCES

Keep Score
○○○○○○○○○○○○○○○○○

FIND THE 16 DIFFERENCES

Keep Score
ooooooooooooooooo

ANSWER KEY

Puzzle Favorites

www.PuzzleFavorites.com

ISBN: 978-1-947676-34-3

   @puzzlefavorites

★ Join! ★

The Puzzle Favorites Club

Sign up now at...
www.PuzzleFavorites.com

Free Printable Puzzles

Coupons

Sneak Peeks

...and More!

ABOUT

Michelle Brubaker is the author and creator of "Magical Land of Sweets & Treats" Spot the Difference Picture Puzzle Book."

As an avid puzzle fan, she also created an entire product line of activity books enjoyed by puzzle enthusiasts around the world.

Please take a quick moment to review this book on Amazon.com and show your support for independent publishers!

★★★★★

Learn How to Publish Your Own Puzzle and Activity Books!

Introducing…. Self-Publishing Courses by Michelle Brubaker the creator and founder of Puzzle Favorites.

➡ Learn more at: www.MichelleBrubaker.com/publishing-courses

Enjoy These Great Titles and More By Puzzle Favorites!

**I Love Mermaids
Spot the Difference Book**

ISBN: 978-1947676329
Amazon: 1947676326

**I Love Shopping
Spot the Difference Book**

ISBN: 978-1947676237
Amazon: 1947676237

**I Love Halloween
Spot the Difference Book**

ISBN: 978-1947676261
Amazon: 1947676261

**I Love Christmas
Spot the Difference Book**

ISBN: 978-1947676251
Amazon: 1947676253

Made in the USA
Monee, IL
26 November 2023